AN ANGRY LETTER IN JANUARY

By the same author:

Drama

Anowa
The Dilemma of a Ghost

Fiction

No Sweetness Here (short stories)
Our Sister Killjoy
Changes

Poetry

Someone Talking to Sometime

Ama Ata Aidoo

AN ANGRY LETTER IN JANUARY AND OTHER POEMS

Dangaroo  Press

Coventry Sydney Aarhus

Acknowledgements

Most of the poems in this volume were earlier individually published in, among others, *The Chapman Review* (Edinburgh); *Echo* (Dakar); *Kunapipi* (Aarhus); *The Literary Review* (Madison, New Jersey); *MS. Magazine* (New York); *West Africa* (London); *South Magazine* (London); *Journal of Gender Issues* (Hull); *Imagine* (Accra). In all instances, it was with the understanding that the author remained the copyright holder.

I would like to thank The Great Lakes Colleges Association (GLCA) of Indiana, Michigan and Ohio for the invitation to be their Fulbright Professor (1988), and the University of Richmond (Richmond, Virginia) for the position of Writer-in-Residence (Spring, 1989). They gave me precious space and time which enabled a number of these poems to get written and platforms for them to be publicly read: in some cases, for the first time.

I would also like to thank Esi Doughan for excellent secretarial services as well as generally, ably and patiently attempting to organise the clearly unorganisable!

The publishers and author wish to thank Ablade Glover for his kind permission to use his painting 'Shanty Town' for the cover.

This book is copyright. Apart from any fair dealing for the purpose of private study, criticism or review, as permitted under the Copyright Act, no part may be reproduced by any process without written permission. Enquiries should be made to the publisher.

© Ama Ata Aidoo 1992

First published in 1992 by Dangaroo Press
Australia: G.P.O. Box 1209, Sydney, New South Wales, 2001
Denmark: Pinds Hus, Geding Søvej 21, 8381 Mundelstrup
UK: 80 Kensington Road, Earlsdon, Coventry CV5 6GH

ISBN 1 871049 27 X
Printed in Great Britain by Villiers Publications, London N6

Contents

As Always, a Painful Declaration of Independence	7
I. *Images of Africa at Century's End*	13
Images of Africa at Century's End	15
In Memoriam: The Ghana Drama Studio	18
A Question From the Expatriate Community	21
An Angry Letter in January	24
Speaking of Hurricanes	26
June 7, 1989 on Tiananmen Square	30
These Days: I	34
Three Poems for Chinua Achebe:	
A Modern African Story	37
Questions	39
New in Africa: I	40
New in Africa: II	41
New in Africa: III	43
Not So New in Africa	45
Loving the Black Angel	47
For Bessie Head	51
On Seeing a Small U.S. Airforce Plane	
at Luanda Airport, June 1987	55
After a Commonwealth Conference	56
No Grief No Joy	58
Compromise	59
An Insider's View	60
Homesickness	62
At Mokador: I	64
At Mokador: II	65
Two Letters:	
Family	66
After an Argument	69

II. Women's Conferences and Other Wonders 71

In Salute to an Enemy of Sorts 73
Just One More Job for Mama 79
Motherhood and the Numbers Game 82
Whom Do We Thank for Women's Conferences? 84
A Young Woman's Voice Doesn't Break. It Gets Firmer 86
Comparisons II: We Women, Still! 88
These Days: II 90
Guest Accommodation 92
Funny Standards 95
July 19, 1991 97
A Path in the Sky 100
3 a.m. and Airborne 102
Even Beans Have Skins! 104
A Birthday Gift 106
A Postcard from My Vacation 107
Back to Square Zero Plus 109
June 7, 1989 110
A Revelation 112
Woman 113

Notes 117

As Always, a Painful Declaration of Independence
– *For Me*

THE PROBLEM

dear friend,
dear comrade,
is not that

I am a woman and
you are a man
– or at least not only that.

Or that
you come from a different quarter of
>the village
>the town
>the district
>the region
>the country
>the continent
>the earth ...

The problem was never that
I am black and you are white
– or not only that.

And much as I wish
I had two whole legs
like you, plus a half,

and given my life,
I could even have done
with an extra arm,

a third eye that saw
not just into me but you
and others and things.

I could have loaned you
a little fat too:
to help you through,

those cold mornings at harmattan
and the even more colder nights
of your winter.

Friend,
height
was not missed much
except when

I needed to reach the
upper shelves of my existence
from where I would want
– occasionally –
to bring down
my forgotten
hopes
aspirations,
plans and projects
to be dusted...

When I would wish, fondly,
that I had one such as you
around
with the long arm that
could elegantly reach for
the tree-tops to
pick
the ripest and most
succulent

successes from the
skies...

Oh My Brother,
the decision to
sever and separate
was not based on the knowledge of me
as a forever dreamer
unable and incapable of handling
the clear world of
take and
take   and
take

while
you could comprehend the
motions of survival and

move with the speed of
a hare in a burning grassland...

I am cutting loose, my dear,
for only one reason:

I do not know
where else you go
whom else you meet
           when we part.

I have had to learn that
these other associations
live:
the connections are
           there and tight
the commitments are real
the allegiances binding.
And the reveberations from them
have a way of

coming at me
shaking my foundations
affecting me
negatively.

I have nightmared of
different gatherings
– after we had parted –
where too
you sit at centre-stage

where they call up
names to censure
characters to assassinate
plot our on-doings.

And

you do not say anything.

You do not own up to

knowing me well or
our comradeship and
what I thought
was our –mutual–
understanding.

So my dear, my love,
I am gone.
I am through.

I cannnot show up for
the meeting tonight or
any other night
anywhere
ever again.

No
My Dear, my friend,

I cannot show up tonight.

I won't be there.

I am gone.

No

My Dear, my friend,

I cannot show up tonight.

I won't be there.

I am gone.

I

IMAGES OF AFRICA AT CENTURY'S END

Images of Africa at Century's End

– *in memoriam Cheikh Anta Diop,*
  and for John Henrik Clarke, Ivan van Sertima,
  Adotey Bing, Aida Brako, Vincent Odamtten
  and by special request,
  Esi Doughan and Kinna Likimani.

Who was it said
The Reason why
you never see
Black Folks properly
e-v-e-r on film or TV
is 'cause White Folks
'find them threatening?!'

Whopei! Abae-o-o-o!

We always thought
our beautiful black skin
          was
      The Problem.

So
Afia and Ola
Eye-leen, Lola and Tapu
bleached and blotched
their skins ugly
to please our masters and our masters' servants.

Now
don't come telling me
flat noses
thick lips and
small ears
must also disappear
to put the world at ease?

That must explain
why The Princess Nefertiti
and the youthful King Tut
were dragged to
Michael Jackson's beauty doctor
long before
Young Michael was born,

and also why
The Sphinx
who looked like
Great Ancestor King Khafre
is being redone!

We should have known
we were in trouble

the day we heard
A Corsican general travelled to Giza
by way of Paris and a crown
to shoot
The Sphinx's nose off
for not-at-all-looking like
his.

Enfin! Helas!! Mon Dieux!!!

Ebusuafo,
for years the
the Sphinx stood
massive eternal
riddled with wisdom and all
very thick-lipped
very flat-nosed.

We never saw him photographed head-on.

But in the year 2020
The New Sphinx would be unveiled

full visage on view
straight nose raised
thin-lips tight
and even, may be, blue-eyed:

a perfect image of the men
who vested so much interest
in his changing face.

You see, *Wekumei*,
when folks figure
you are their slave
your past belongs to them.

And mind you, The Man will try
                to grab our future too.

Shall we let him?

In Memoriam:
The Ghana Drama Studio

- *For Robert McLaren, who is committed to
  the struggle and to drama, and
  Efua T. Sutherland, who birthed.*

When you asked me
whether I felt at home
coming back here,
I first shuddered,

remembering that actually,
The Ghana Drama Studio
was not pulled down.
It was uprooted.

By the time I got there
– just a few days before your question –
they had filled the monstrous hole
the operation left.

The Ancients had said that
Home
is where your shrines flourish.
And the Ghana Drama Studio had been
my shrine...of sorts.

I couldn't have called it a
white elephant.

It was just an equally rare
white gazelle
which slept under the city nims,
away from the tropical morning glare,

but
poised,
always,
for a cue
to spring into swift precise action.

But The Drama Studio is gone, Robert,
razed to the ground:
to make way for someone's notion of
the kind of theatre
I
should
want.

When you asked me
whether I felt at home returning
here,
I wondered how an old campaigner like
you
could have asked the question which
I had learnt – sadly – to expect
from the friendly
        but chatty taxi drivers who
bring me home here in Harare,
                ... and elsewhere.

And the forever pain around my heart
jumped, roaring for attention.

Because Comrade,
(holy places and their desecrations aside,
and not to mention the sacred duty
to feel at home anywhere in Africa,
and love every little bit of this
battered and bartered continent which
I still, perhaps naively,
call my own,)

I had thought folks like you n' me
had stopped
defining Home
from way way back,
and have
calmly assumed that

'Home'
can also be anyplace anywhere
where someone or other
is not trying to

fry your mind,

roast your arse, or

waste you and yours altogether.

Hm???

A Question
From the Expatriate Community

– *To Kari Dako, for her good-natured cynicism, and
Kinna (IX), for her edification!*

Apropos something or other that
I cannot remember, and
smug in the plans for her own future,

she had asked me
with a frankness born of long friendship
– and short memory, deliberately cultured –

whether
I can see myself
growing old
here?

And I remember you and your clear views on
Ghanaian emigres
the whole world over:

forever
postponing life and living
as we ready ourselves for a beckoning old age
when, as elders of the clan and
our hairs dyed beyond infant black,

we shall sit...
after   'a little something in the morning,'
   'a little something at noon,'
   'a little something in the evening,'

...admired by siblings and other
ancillary brothers and sisters who
could never have done as well as we

since they stayed at home:

...and held with due respect in the caring arms of
their offspring
our grateful neices and nephews
to whom we dispense
our black-market-supported
favours and wisdoms.

Both – the hard currency and the experience –
acquired from
unspeakable humiliations
in other people's lands.

We shall try then not to remember
the daily insults:
promotions denied,
our children having to move on to
harsher climates
in pursuit of education.

Since, as the dependants of foreigners,
– forget how high their grades or
                            how keen their desire –
they simply
cannot get into
the army   or
schools for would-be
doctors
engineers
lawyers.

Our Wife,
the list of exclusions is very long.

But mind you,
all African countries treat
all other Africans
                            from beyond their borders

like shit,
                     or at best, as
flotsam and jetsam.

'My friend,
where were you all this time?
I was asking if you can see yourself
growing old here?'

In my mind's eye,
the image of me as
the adored elder of the clan
receeds
          receeds

                 disappers.

I do not tell my friend
what I was thinking.   That
if what I am feeling now is not old age already,
then frankly,
it signifies little
where the real thing finds me.

I shall be beyond caring:

an unprepared
            un-secured
                      wanderer...

'In any case,' I remind her,

'such questions are
meaningless for those
who are not at all sure
they have a choice.'

An Angry Letter in January

Dear Bank Manager,

I have received your letter.
Thank you very much:
threats,
intimidations, and all.

So what,
if you wont give me a loan
of two thousand?
Or only conditioned by
special rules
 and regulations?

Because I am   *not*

white
male   *or*
a 'commercial farmer'?

(And in relation to the latter,
whose land is this anyway?)

I know that but for what I am not,
you could have signed
 away
two solid millions, and
not many questions asked.

Of course I am angry.

Wouldn't you be if you were me?

Reading what you had written
was enough

to spoil for me
all remaining eleven months of the year,
plus a half.

But I wont let it.

I had even thought
of asking God
that the next time round,
He makes me
white, male, and a 'commercial' farmer.

But I wont.

Since apart from
the great poverty
                    and
the petty discriminations,

I have been happy
being me:

an African
a woman
and a writer.

Just take your racism
            your sexism
                    your pragmatism
                                off me;

overt
    covert or
            internalised.

And
damn you!

Speaking of Hurricanes
– *for Micere Mugo and all other African exiles.*

I

My Sister,

Have you noticed how
around August/September
every year,

Africa
gathers her storms and
hurls them across the Atlantic to
the poor Americas
                and the poorer Caribbean:
Gilbert, Sullivan, Victor, Hugo...

blustering, savage, masculine?...

Ow,w,w,...
the ruination they leave behind!
levelled homes
torn cables
poisoned water, and
too many lives snuffed out or at best
broken.

Just reckoning the damage is a
whirlwind of sorts.

And we almost thought:
'how clever of Africa !'

Until we looked around us, and
stopped short on our way to jubilation.

II

See!

Africa had always kept
the more interesting of
the commotions for herself.

Years of economic and political tornadoes
                        on our courtyards
centuries-old gales that
blew our hopes
up, down, left, right:
anywhere and everywhere... except
forward to fulfilment.

We know tyrannical and despotic
winds that whisked away some of
our ablest bodies and strongest minds to

our conquerors' doorsteps,

where they
cut cane
pick cotton and
real garbage.

These days, they sit.
African men sit.
Able bodies strong minds and all,
guarding private property or
staring at nothing at all. While

African women in various forms of
civilised bondage are
still and forever wiping
baby snot and adult shit:
bourgeois black or imperial white.

Who cares?!

III

The Slave Trade was only
a chapter, a watershed perhaps, but
really no more than an episode in the hands of
a master tale-performer who knows too well, how
to change the story,
its telling,
its music,
its drums

to suit his times.

But speaking of very recent events, My Sister,
have you met any of
the 'post-colonial' African political refugees
shuffling on the streets of
London
Paris
Washington
Stockholm and
The Hague?

Minds – and bodies – discarded
because they tried
to put themselves to good use?

Please,
don't tell me how lucky they are.

They know. We know.

They are the few who got away

...escaped
the secret governments and
their secret cabinets,
the secret cabinets and

their secret agendas for
the secret meetings out of which come
secret decisions, laws, decrees, orders from
secret army to secret police for
secret arrests
secret torture and
secret death.

IV

Ow My Sister, let me lament
my openly beautiful land and her people
who hide good things and bad so well,
only decay and shame become
public,
international.

All storms are dangerous.

But I fear most
the ones I can't see
whose shrieking winds are
not heard around the world
      and
the havoc they wreak
cannot even be discussed.

June 7, 1989 on Tiananmen Square

– *for Baby Ekua Marguerite Prah: (I)*

I

My sister,

in the long run,
the question is
not
whose definitions of what hold
whose story gets told   or
how much.

And trust me, My Sister, beyond such
collective certainty,
there is very little else – o!

Mo Nua, the question really is:
after a millennia in a coma
when do we wake up?

We have
slept through too much and too long...

We slept
through great commotions of
shrieking virgins at their raping
young warriors at their beheading
all survivors enslaved
at home and especially
abroad.

II

We slept
as our own relatives led the thieves into our
home, and threw open the gates
                              to our treasures.

Vandals took our gods,
placed them where
inspiration oozed from their wooden pores
to infuse wonder into
the art of their great masters, while
the raiders threw
departing darts of disdain
and proclaimed how
unendowed and destitute
we were:

'– quite primitive really,' they said.

We slept while
our conquerors returned to dynamite
our mountains and our pyramids and
take out whatever could/can be took
– which was always considerable –
                              and is,

and they return
again and again and again and again
                              and again...

My Sister, we sleep.

We still sleep
like the python that swallowed
                  the elephant while
the children's bellies bloat with starvation.

III

Nana used to tell us how
if we were good and crouched
                by the family hearth,
we shall be
safe from
the wild beasts' fangs
the slave raiders' guns, their
                torches and their ropes.

So,
where do we hide from
our brothers and our sisters
who crouch by the family hearth   with their
high-tech torture things   and
rapid firearms

consumed by their own fears, and desire
only
to protect the power
we freely gave them or
they took?

Now
the boys from the old neighborhood
        – our playmates –
turn into wolves and lions
        – right before our eyes –
to people our forests   and
return terror into our lives...

...do you remember, My Sister,
  – we played *gotta-gotta*?
  – we played *ampe*?

Mo Nua,
we still sleep

here in foreign lands,
away from the uncertainties
             at home,
free
    to dance
           to sing
                 to eat
all we can of
buttered bread, bacon and
                baked beans...

Yet,
this time and even in
these places,
we sharpen our knives in sleep,
to cut the tongues of our children,
put blinkers on their eyes,
block their ears with molten lead...

Indeed,

like the man's true sambos, we
giggle,
      leer, and
              cavort around
in orgasmic glee,

as we ourselves
take the brains of our children out, and
stuff their heads with
cottonwool.

My Sister, the question is   not
who defines democracy for whom,   but

after a millennia in a coma,
when do we wake up?

Mo Nua, when shall we wake up?

These Days: I
– *for Baaba Roberts*

Little Sister,
keep calm,
relax.

Moboso gya. Mammbohwe wo nkwan m'.

It couldn't have been too long
                    ago that
asking
where anyone was
whom we had not seen in years
meant nothing more than
a goodwilled curiosity,
a wanting to know
how the family – close and extended – is,
a way to catch up with The Home News:

– the young women and men
    of the house, which got married
    and to whom;
– who has had children, how many and when;
– which children are in school, in training,
                where and how they do;

– and news of prosperous times,
    promotions
    businesses expanding
    houses getting built
    whether they sank the much
                – needed well in
    the neighborhood, and
    brought light –
    – good shining light to
    our mother's doorstep?

– and the bad news too
which we don't need but must have...

>Oh Dear Little Sister
>things must have changed
>so much so suddenly.
>
>They must have.
>They must have.
>How they must have!
>
>Or
>I should not have read
>such panic in your voice,
>just by asking
>how Big Sister does.

So what, if she is still at home?

When did home stop being the place to be?
When did being at home become
proof of failure?
a life gone wrong?

Should we all fly away?

>Wander?
>
>>Get lost?

Little Sister, your voice
tells me
what I dare not
see
hear
know:

that
these days,

home is
what we fear most;
where we think they are,
who can go
nowhere else;

where we get buried while
we wait to die.

Poor us, My Little Sister,
poor us.

Three Poems for Chinua Achebe

A MODERN AFRICAN STORY

Yes,
strange as it may sound,
it is true.

I got deported this morning from
my home, my village, my country and the land which
my forefathers and foremothers bled for,
                                    and tilled
from the beginning of time.

My crime?

I look like My Cousin from across the border, and
His President and My Prime Minister
do not see
eye to eye.

Mind you,
My Brother the Professor protests that
theoretically and linguistically,
'it simply doesn't make sense!
No one can ever be deported from
                        their native country.'

I was packing as he was talking.

I had no time to stop and tell him to look
around:

in a land where
former freedom fighters
are vagrants, or buy respectability only

by guarding the property for those they mortgaged
their youths to fight against,
the factories and the homes they crawled
at night – in the good old days – to burn...

one can be deported from one's birthplace.

And
I
was.

This morning.

QUESTIONS

– *for us, 'Today's So-Called African Leadership'*

They say all beings fight to live:

the mole
the lion and
the crow.

They say all creatures must fight to be

in the air
on land
in water.

And as for human you and me

we shoot like wild mushrooms
– in the dark –
sneak up like snakes
claw like cats
pounce and trample,

conquer
kill
consume.

Then just go limp: again
like wild mushrooms
– at high noon.

So where do We come in
Who feel bad just to be firm?
damn all else?
do our own nasty thing or two?

And surely,
500 hundred years is too long
to take the kicks
without a murmur?

For what
do we still come
with cup in hand,
begging,
pleading and
endlessly shifting?

Who would have us be human
in a world
of cruel beasts and
even more cruel men?

How dare we trust
when Trust took a vacation
			– several million years ago – and
never bothered to come back?

Put quite simply,
in whose name do we ever act?

Whose tomorrow do we sell?

NEW IN AFRICA: I

Was Pliny serious
when he said:
'out of Africa always comes something new.'?

Shamwari, since he couldn't have foreseen,
he couldn't have meant the last 500 years:

when
Time closed in on itself   and
Europe closed in on us,   and
the only new things
we served ourselves   and
our enemies dished to us
were very old potions:

– nearly always violent –and
just warmed over
every one hundred years or so.

As for Africa herself,
conquered
raped
re-conquered
re-raped,

She wriggles still.

So we also struggle on
– clear eyed or blind –
sometimes with song,
often with dance,

and always,
with a prayer on our lips.

New in Africa: II

When soldiers get tired of wielding power and
declare how looting is gone sour;

when soldiers stand ready to confess
knowing they'll get fired or much much worse

there's something new in Africa.

Child of the Land,
not so loud or a whisper.

Sometimes in Africa,
things go age-ing before flower-ing

Child of the Land, not so loud.
At least, not yet.

New in Africa: III

Wen
civilian
shon soja-town

stop
whisperin with
dem curtains down,

sometin new dey w'Africa.

Listen to the ocean
washing castle walls:
where a king was jailed
on his way to exile.
Strangers came to beat our drums,
strangers beat our drums.

Promise
thick wads of money notes
sweet Mama's smoky smell,

fat bank accounts
in distant lands,
when the coup is over.

Too bad, Boys,
if you are caught,
shot by plotters from

The Other Side,
grinning victory
waving The Flag...

wen civilia ron from barrack-door,
neba neba to retorn
new life be here in Africa.

Listen to the ocean
washing castle walls
where a king was jailed
on his way to exile.
Strangers beat our family drums,
strangers beat our drums.

Not So New in Africa
– *for Fela Anikulapo-Kuti*

Was it Koo the Fisherman or
Kurai the Farmer

who remarked, somewhat wrily,
that the trouble with neo-colonialism is that
we have to cope with the same crimes, but
there are no colonial sergeants to drill
their own criminals and ours?!

He must have referred to
the current human flood from
European Houses of Correction to our homes.

And you remember, don't you, that
it was part of the cruel clarities of those days
that they called them 'prisons',
and everyone knew
which side of the gate everyone stood?

Now, freed from their internal exile, and
rejected by Canada or Australia or
some such once-open-but-now-closed places,
they make for our continent: to
one or other of our ridiculous tea-cuppy states

– the inefficiences are the same, and
so is the fear of the white man –

Otherwise, My Brother,
where else but in Africa
would you meet a Weiss-Schmidt with
a most pronounced Yorkshire burr, or
a singing Italian called McPherson?

And we still call them 'Sir.'
And we call them 'Lady.'

Loving the Black Angel
– *for Ben Moloise, Alex La Guma and Our Other Fallen Heroes.*

I always knew
I loved Lucifer.

Don't ask me
why or
how.

Was he not the first rebel?
a champion
who would not
grin grovel scrape creep or
kiss
the original white arse?

Ah, kinsmen and friends,
help me hail my princely fighter
who
betrayed kings and class, and
gleefully smashed a
thousand glittering crowns.

Loving Lucifer should be
easy:
for
his spirit that refuses to get drenched in
stolen milk and
extorted honey...

...and in any case,
was he not rough, and hairy, and...
pitch black?

Is he not
my enemies' enemy

with plenti promis to be my fren'?
An ally come to
toughen my arm as
I seize thunderbolts
from the earth and skies to
smash crush and reduce sweetly-smug slave-drivers to
smithereens?

I just love Lucifer
daring doing dancing
through
waterjets
teargas and
other great open mouths whose
only mission is

forever death.

I certainly should love Lucifer
who refuses to
'take things as they are,'

to whom dissent
with a racist hangman's rope
seems prettier than
touched-pictures of
'the new African bourgeoise.'

'Hold up the photo for better light, my good
neighbour – you know we are already rather dark –
and my dear, as you know, everything in there is
the best that a black man can have
under the circumstances.'

They cut you down, Comrade,
and sent your spirit out.
But who says I want another angel
in my already hot heaving heaven?

Don't you see
in teeming celestial camps and
down among the ancestors,
multitudes of relentless impi
forever fighting
as our heroes must?

So
You, La Guma,
You Moloise, and
All You Beautifully Young Deers
whose lives
the real devil daily
snaps:

don't sleep.

As you join the ancestors

don't sleep.

Stay awake.

Keep alert.

For the battle continues.
The struggle clearly continues,
and we must fight:
You below
us above:
until nothing stands
nothing at all stands
that has to fall.

So that
We can rebuild
our lives
our hopes
our cities of gold.

O, I just love you,
Lucifer.

For Bessie Head

To begin with,
there's a small problem of address:

calling you
by the only name some of us
knew you by,

hailing you by titles
you could not possibly
have cared for,

referring you to
strange and clouded
origins that eat into
our past our pain
like prize-winning cassava tubers in
abandoned harvest fields...

Some of us never ever met you.

And who would believe
that but those who know
the tragedies of our land
where
non-meetings,
visions unopening   and other such
abortions are
every   day   reality?

To continue a
confession of sorts,

'Miss Head' will just not do.
'Bessie' too familiar
Bessie Head,

your face swims into focus
through soft clouds of
cigarette smoke and from behind the
much much harder barriers erected by some
quite unbelievable
20th. century philosophy,

saying more of
your strength
than all the tales
would have us think.

For the moment,

we fear and
dare not accept that
given how things
are,

poetry almost becomes
dirges and
not much more.

But
we hold on to knowing
ourselves as daughters of
darklight women
who are so used to Life
– giving it
feeding it –

Death
was always
quite unwelcome:
– taking them by surprise –
an evil peevish brat
to be flattered,
cleaned
oiled

pomaded
over-dressed and perfumed...

We fear to remember:
fatigued as we are by so much
death and dying and
the need to bury and
to mourn.

Bessie Head:
such a fresh ancestress!

If you chance
on a rainy night
to visit,

if you chance
on a sunny day
to pass by,

look in to see
– how well we do
– how hard we fight
– how loud we scream

against the plots
– to kill our souls our bodies too
– to take our land, and
– feed us shit.

Come
benevolently,
Dear Fresh Spirit,

that rejoining
The Others,
you can tell them
now more than ever,

do we need
the support
the energy

to create
recreate and
celebrate...

nothing more
absolutely
nothing less.

On Seeing a Small U.S. Airforce Plane at Luanda Airport, June 1987

We stopped breathing
a hair's breath of time.

Our eyes broke through their curtains and
wrung their hands
over our heads.

Our tongues
curled in on themselves,
rolled into small dark corners, and
turned leaden.

But

the plane could have been
on a mission of
friendship?
ordinary commerce?
old-fashioned peace?

So
hello dread and
friendly panic,

where
do you two come from?

After a Commonwealth Conference
– *for Kinna III*

Because

you are here
to remind me to be grateful to
– it must be The Lord –
for small mercies,

I shall not
wail
shave my hair or
do another fasting trip at the dawn of a
day that has put more bile on my tongue.

But Child,
out there where
our thousands are dying and
our millions
do not have food to
choose to eat or
not,

how does one tell the story of men
who are nothing at all, and
leaders who are only
skilled in the art of
anti-people treachery?

Child,
I hear you: and since
wisdom
does not always grow with our grey hairs,

may be,
you can tell me

56

what to do with
my shame, and

Our Continent once more
betrayed?

No Grief No Joy

There is
no joy no grief
when
generals lie ill
from
mosquito bites or quake with fear at the prospect of
just
saying 'no' to
a guilty thief.

There is no mourning
no grieving when
mild resolves come
dancing in full battle gear.

There is only
confusion and
shame...

...and fear for what another day might bring.

Compromise

I.

We could always
have done
worse:

supporting
meaningless words and
fear of action
with
nigger reasoning and
sambo logic.

II. (Haiku)

We could have done worse:
talk talk no – deeds nigger shu
ffle sambo logic.

An Insider's View

– for Kinna VI

Even a self-imposed exile is
another prison.

I opened the gate,
banged it shut on myself, and
threw the key away.
Or just misplaced it.

I thought I could get
that key again and easily
if only I could find some time, and
carefully look.

But in this nightmare world of:

Aliens Compliance Orders
Temporary Work Permits
regular applications for regular visas
permanent residence requirements
Green Cards,
                Red Cards and
                              Blue...

...And not to mention:

just learning to cope
in places where
I cannot take anything at all for granted,

we know that
other doors out of this prison are open
                      all the time.

But they only lead to *suminado*:
the backyard
the outhouses
the fields beyond.

So of course
I can run all I want. To
other lands other exiles.

Going home is another story.

Homesickness
– *for Anna Rutherford*

This afternoon,

I bolted from
the fishmarket:

my eyes smarting with
shame
at how too willingly and sheepishly
my memory had slipped up
after the loss of my taste buds.

– Just like an insecure politician creaming up
              to his boss.

Familiarly in an unfamiliar land,
so strong and so sweetly strong,
the smells of the fish of
my childhood hit hard and soft,
wickedly musky.

All else fall into focus
except the names of the fish.

While from distant places in my head
The Atlantic booms and roars or
calmly creeps swishing foam on the hot sand.

But I could not remember their *Fantse* names.

They were labelled clearly enough
            – in English –
which
tragically
brought no echoes...

One terrifying truth
unveiled in one short afternoon:

that
exile brings losses like
forgetting to remember
ordinary things.

Mother,
when next we meet,
I shall   first   bring you
your truthspeaker's stone:

the names and tastes of fish are also
simple keys to unlock
secret sacred doors.

And I wail to foreign far away winds:

Daughter of my Mother and my Father's Orphan,
what is to become of me?

And Those like me?

At Mokador: I

The weatherman did not tell us
how warm it was going to be, or not.

But I know by the look of things
it's surely gonna rain today.

That sign is not bad.
Oh, not at all.

But then there is also a
chill wind blowing through my heart,

while watching and 'jealous-ing,
no small',
three young brothers
– who at a pinch could be my sons –
calmly quaff frosted beer at
9 in the morning,

to still
what fears of what failures or what faults?
to gain
what courage in the face of...to face what?

So
I think to myself that may be, if
I could also drink beer at
9 in the morning,

may be...
may be...

At Mokador: II

I can feel
misery coiling around my mind
like a tapeworm
from the stream outside our village,

which
both
the white governor and
the black president

had refused
to inspire us to
clean out, dam up, and
plant sweet-smelling flowers along its banks.

Now, I just sit here,
getting screamed at by a
pimply drop-out from some Aegean island, and
wondering where

on the markings of this tapeworm
do my different concerns begin and end

for myself
the family smaller and larger
all our people
– at home
– abroad?

Two Letters

FAMILY

To Baby Ekua Marguerite Prah: III
– from Kalamazoo, Michigan, USA., as I watch
a group of our younger relatives
'just talking' on a Saturday afternoon.

My dear Sister,

We have truly
come a long way
to be here.

Trudging the paths of

Bush negroes
House-and-Field Niggers
Wanting-to-pass Octoroons, and

all other colours between
glistening black and
glaring light;

Non-Immigrants
dragged here in chains;
New immigrants
pulled here by
the economics of
The New (est) World Order!

Sister
from this sample crop of our tomorrow:
I see:

one
vulnerable golden nymph,
fighting against engulfing disillusionment
silent, suspicious, watchful;

right by her is she
of the squeaky laughter by the lagoon where
the muddied waters of
old African confidence and
the modern sea of
America's ethnic bewilderments
meet;

facing those two is
she who
along with her generation of
our continent's
multi - origin-ed
multi - loco-ed
children,
struggles grimly but cheerfully,
today as yesterday to
keep her head, and her voice (!) above
so many waters;

finally, look at their *nuabanyin*
an original Atlas
a giant of warm
smooth blackness
laughing outside while
wailing inside against
history's most paradoxical
invisibility.

Oh my dear Sister,

I had no intention when I began this letter,
of depressing you or myself.

So, to be continued.

Yours truly,...

AFTER AN ARGUMENT
– *for Henry Moyana*

Dear Henry,

The issue is not that
as friends
you advocate capitalism, and
I trust socialism.

Ndugu,
the tragedy is:
that as Africans
we feel compelled to take sides;

that if there is
an exit
from
collective
decay and distress
we have not
found it yet;

that, by the way,
'A Mixed Economy' is
definitely,
decidedly,

Not It.

'Every choice bears a price,
Not choosing costs thrice,'
said The Ancients.

Trust them to know!

II

WOMEN'S CONFERENCES AND OTHER WONDERS

In Salute to an Enemy of Sorts
– *for Efua Eduawa, my 'Little Sister.'*

...and now, let us sing of good old roaches.

I

Their forest types came
out of the dry cornfields:
clean,
but still harried. Like their city relatives.

Then
they were there:
hiding among the old silks and velvets that
Mother dragged into the sunlight
along with the other heirlooms

– the papers for the gold-mining concessions that
no one else had bothered to pursue after
The One-and-Only Enterprising Grand Uncle
who had secured it had passed on –

farms abandoned to grateful croppers and
the anxiously waiting-to-claim-their-own
forests...
pits of palm oil gone to wax
                gone to wax
                        gone to clear wax!

Little Sister, are you really sure
you never heard the story?

About how the year after
the Long-necked White Prince came and judged
Our Grandmothers' palm oil the clearest of the land,

and therefore the best to send overseas to make soap
to care for and perfume our ladies' skins,
the price of palm oil fell so much
it flowed freer and cheaper
than the waters of the Okyi River in flood?

So Grandfather designed the oil pits
to wait for a better season that
never came again
                        in his lifetime.

That's The How of the palm oil wax pits...

Little Sister, are you really sure
You never heard the story?

Well, I did...
...And ask Wofa.

There is not a single family like ours
in all of the Guinea Coast or beyond for
                        letting go of wealth.

(Except Nana Yamoa,
who made a fortune,
built a house inside an orchard,   or
built an orchard around his house,
where they say each tree got taken care of
better than his new brides...

Big Mother claims that
even the ground beneath
the custard apples and the oranges were swept
every morning of every Friday.

...Of course, in the process, he made more money.
Good money.

Though for his trouble,
he got a few bullets through his head which
blew his life out in a flash,
one early Friday morning...

...another very long story, Little Sister,
another very very long story...)

The roaches were always there:
in the corners of the frontroom where
the unwashed pots and pans stood, and

they survived the heat from beneath
the bamboo *apa* where
corn and other goodies were hung
to smoke and keep until next year's harvest.

II

The cockroaches were there
in the university bungalow
even though
orderliness
cleanliness   and
thin bodies were mandated trinity for
winning lust from men and
respect from colleagues...
...Or some claimed.

And then in
New York and New Orleans,
I found the biggest and the boldest roaches of them all:
– with sweet American bluff and bluster,
– totally unafraid,
– more confident than the guys on Wall Street,
– long-bodied and agile like basket-ball players,
– aggressive and slippery like hockey men on ice.

No timid artists and apologetic academics in sight.

And the females were uniformly brown:

naturally – as now in most cases –
or
bestowed by the sun on those
who can afford that kind of tan
in winter and all other weather,
or
outside the great legs swathed in coffee sheer,
coaxed with cream, and
other marvels of modern scientific technology
to yield a whiter or browner face
depending on where on the rainbow you stood,
or
given as gifts by more high-tech, but kindly, through
specially-designed colours
incorporated into the latest photo films...
so that pale-faces can look
instantly and attractively
brown,
while you and I turn out
darker than we really are...

Perhaps, Little Sister,
what we see are not exactly our colors shining thru!!!

...another very very long story...

III

Now,

hiding somewhat in this
cute colonial legacy for which
I cannot afford the rent,

where
the water pours and pours and pours out of taps, while
I try hard not to think of Aisha stooping and scraping
the bottom of a well that dried
                      before her mother was born,

but also here in this lovely quadrangle
where to my delight,
the trees and the shrubs stay evergreen and clipped,
              watered daily by Johnny mind you
                      except when it rains...

Yes, even here,
cockroaches
make my days a misery, and
my evenings a nightmare.

They are still smart:
toddlers in their thousands,   and
youths like those I see
dropping out and dropping back into education
or reggae-crazed
but still not joking at all
about life,

while once in a while,
a tired matriach emerges,
her breathing pride perched sassily
like her woollen cap in the cold,

inspite of the attempts to beat her down:

– viciously, racially, sexually, by the colonists.
– viciously, fondly, for her own good, by her dad.
– viciously, with love, to submission, by her man.

Yet still a wild thing, hand firm on
her basket-weave, her crochet...

IV

And so back to batan, My Little Sister.

Drenched in all brands of insecticide:
cheap, expensive, perfumed,
you must have heard how these days
some even claim their death-delivering products to be
'earth-friendly'?!

So I watch them still
in their bruised but swaggering multitudes,
– like Ashantis rising from
an English genocidal military expedition
                    to their shrines and palaces, or
groups of bruised but rude and defiant Fantis
brushing off from their bottoms
a pacification exercise by the
British West African Frontier Force.

They too work hard at surviving:
very very hard.
So I salute them, and
calmly surrender.

Just One More Job for Mama

– *for Kinna VII*

'Ajumako ampesi wobo kaw dzi'*

'The most difficult science on earth is human engineering.' –
F.K. Buah

My Dear Young Woman,

You know how
I have cut and polished
guilt
into a great and luminous
art...

on account of
your failings?

your genuine forgetfulnesses?
your pretended lapses of memory and
other faculties?

So, may be
it was really my fault.

I should
not only have remembered
to let you know
but also
kept reminding
you
over, and over and over again.

That:

– I swear by my wounded knee
mara mondue, –

It's
not only in America
there is no free lunch.

There
isn't
wasn't and
can't be

ANY free lunch
EVEN in Ajumako.

'They told us
Our fathers told us
They told us.'

For,
even out there
where
the savannah is
still dotted in places with
good timber,
and
on a clear day
the Atlantic melts and shines
teeming with good herrings in August from
bays, coves, capes and reefs,
where
the poisonous wastes from
our masters' backyards
have not got to them yet(?), and

there are still coconut trees
for which no one really cares
to claim
ownership...

...yes, even in Ajumako

THERE IS NO FREE LUNCH.

So Child,
if someone,
– my friend or yours –

remembers that
you
exist and
decides on any day for some reason
to
send
you
a book
some b-r-e-a-d
a card to say
hello, or
just plain old-fashioned love,

stop a while
– considering no one owes you
anything at all – and
say a little

'Thank you.'

Please?

Please?

PLEASE?

Motherhood and the Numbers Game
– *for Kinna VIII*

'Now
that I am suffering so much,
I know I am truly a mother,'

said
Egyeifi to the other screaming
woman.

2 painfully hoarse voices
still managing to bellow like
cows in an abattoir;
4 veins swollen to
sizes larger then the
2 necks they stood on.

'meda w'ase
meda w'ase
meda w'ase...

osiande,
ama meehu de,
saana moso
maawo!'*

I always marvelled at the
non – logic
of it all,

and even managed
the educated lady's dainty grin
the day
they told me that in all the
20 years I was away,

my mother never slept a wink!

The woman who spoke
– my mother's friend –
stared straight into my eyes
bespectacled already
as, it seems,
all eyes must be
20/20 visioned or not, when
folks turn 40 at the very least.

So
at 2 in the morning
I lie here in the dark
more sharp-eyed than
the cat my totem:

anxious
angry
sleepless –

blissfully anxious
happily angry and
nervously fulfilled

that

I
too
am
a mother!

Whom Do We Thank for Women's Conferences?

Here
in this truly
no man's land,

all is fair as understood not in terms of
Penelope's false blondness but
that which is right and healthy.

Where
we throw
our big
hairy legs and
bottoms that make any Levis cry for air.

Hairy too are the faces
we acknowledge
– some were born that way – or
as signs of:
the pills we took in,
the wombs we threw out,   and
plain
normal
ageing.

Yet

ancient graces
walk elegantly tall or
charmingly petite
in celebration pinks and royal indigos...
as though the earth itself was
newly found,
the air a discovery.

We were not afraid of ideas.
Not our own.
Not those of others.

Along those corridors and
in those easy days' assemblies,
apologizing for our being was
not on.

We were
Nobody's wives or mistresses.

No one called us
    'Mother':
and when some daughters present did,
it was with the clearest mandate   that
they picked the fight where we brought it.

We were
only ourselves:
each alone as when we were born, and
shall be, when
we died.

But
living and together,
a true power thing that
searches
researches
solving
resolving...

And as always
sweetly hopeful as
only women can be.

A Young Woman's Voice Doesn't Break. It Gets Firmer
– *for Kinna IV*

I remember
you at four
seven or
eleven,

your baby voice:
both real and pretend
telling me
(or rather whining slightly)
how you missed me, and
who had done what to you or said,
while I
had been away...

Now
your voice
comes briskly along the wires,
through the air waves and
over the earth

reporting
how alright everything
at home is, and
ordering me to
just relax
and be about the business
I travelled
all the way here for.

And clearly,
if you missed me,
you were not half about to let on.

Young woman,

– for I dare not call you 'Child' anymore –
may be
when we are into
our normal existences with
their needs and their tensions,

I do not notice the
changes that
take place in you.

But when
I am away and
the phones permit,
I do.

The measures of your growth
knock confidently at the
       doors of my perception
announcing themselves in
more than certain terms.

Of course,
we only speak of a data of
one.

But
if yours
is anything to go by,

then surely,
as she grows
from child into woman,

a girl's voice doesn't break:
it gets firmer.

Comparisons II: We Women, Still!

Honestly, Sisters,

there is some elation here
...and some bitterness too.

But if you want to find out
how equal
            even
the more equal 1/2 of us are,
come see us at any
public library

– after a normal 9-5 working day.

We are there
in our numbers:
multi-racial
multi-national
multi-ethnic.

All middle class of course.

And therefore,
fat.

But since fat is out
                    for the femmes fatales,
The Grease
these days,
is often in the bones,
not on!

– and indulged. Like
favorite house-mice

scurrying through
the catalogues and
chumping up the bookshelves on
what was left

after the feast of the masters:

desperately hopeful too,
that
one day,
over-fed on crumbs but
armed with knowledge

we shall be permitted to
catch on:
lost momentum
lost hopes
lost plans
...life itself...

And our not-so-priviledged sisters?

Honey,
they are
still at it: after even a
normal 9-5 working day:

taken up with
what's waiting of the
brutal loads that were
their lives and most painfully
abandoned,

before, long before 9 this morning.

These Days:II

– *for Hilary Homans*

Last night
I could not help but recall
how Mother ended
those precious lessons in
personal grooming:

'... and remember
to keep a cheerful face:
it costs nothing, and
will do you no end of good.'

Last night,
staring in the face of
that
special
plague
which
   – the ancients must have foretold –
shall come to
end all human hopes,

You and I
discovered
   – if we hadn't before –

that these days,
a cheerful face is
a hard commodity to come by.

And we moaned about a ruined world
doubly ruined
for our children
by

epidemics of rolling tanks
scuds,
other missile sorties and
the glee of
foolish old men
cheering at skies
exploding into
flowery flames
to
rain
death
      destruction
               despair.

So
it was not easy.
But we tried
        very hard
                to go shopping for
laughter,

as another lightning ripped
through
the darkening air.

Guest Accommodation

People have passed through this house:
at different hours
perhaps mostly odd.

Dozens and dozens of
– most especially – men, and
perhaps a few women,
mostly white,
that without a doubt,
perhaps one or two black.

So, here,
we hug greetings in
the collective human odour of
hurried respite from
ordinary
– ever so human – concerns, to
ordinary ever-so-human concerns.

The pillows talk of
many heads:
their scalps frozen in the winters;
the roots of
their hairs melting in the summers.

The taps drip endlessly.

The boards
            crack
                 creak
                      croak
around and under.

Both
the belaboured breathing of the boiler

then, and its
relieved laughter now
explode and echo through
these rooms...

Waiting to be exorcised,
the ghost that is me and
those of others like me
go up and down the stairs,
pace the corridors
walk the rooms
the whole night through!

Do you remember
Raul of Mexico?
A brilliant neuro-something-or-other?
Anxiously enthusiastic and
full of youthful crimes and
confessions?

Of course,
We know.
He and I and those like us.

We know we are the chosen few:
plucked from the miseries of our
impoverished and
decaying lands, to

come and
help
already shining lives to
glow.

So
we sweat
our confusions into
these sheets and these pillows.

Birds of brief passage,

We soon leave
This House to
The Old and Native Ghosts who
blissfully
hum and haw their way
through

fridges,
boilers,
radiators.

Funny Standards

– for my brother B.K.Hagan, in memoriam.

I was only this high, when
they told me
– with that very serious voice
    grown-ups get
when they speak to children –

that
you always passed
'with flying colours
the true test of a complete gentleman'.

'He can eat a whole pot of
palmnut oil stew or soup
without
spotting his *white* shirt, even once!'

B.K.,
now that
I am as old as they then were
    – if not older – and
maybe, can, perhaps, possibly
judge
the kind of person you must have been,

I suspect
you couldn't have given a damn for
their colonial penny or neo-colonial pesewa
what such ideas stood for.

I suspect
you
simply
liked white shirts:
– wore them

– lived in them
palm soups and stews and all...

In any case,
I would rather
you
were
here
My Brother My Prince:

still
loving the kids you so expertly
taught from their first day in your
classroom, and
groomed so well to leave
your hands at year's end,

your prime brain
not fed to maggots in its prime,
and
your voice,
your wit...

July 19, 1991
– for Maggie Matowe, and all others out there like her

Truly,
My Dear Sister,
the original phoenix
must have been a woman –
– of your sort:

in
body
mind...and
spirit too.

So I sit and stare at some
truths in the face
– this among others.

Reminding myself of
a time and place
'so near and so far away'

when and where
body spirit shattered and
the mind a little less than
its normal dear incomplete self –

I had thought of writing a
poem,

– and put a great deal of effort
        into it –

about
rising from fires and ashes,
legs, necks and colour of skin
intact,

or some such notion to cheer up
a sinking self in a
hospital that was itself sinking
                    into the sea!!!

I can already hear
the beginning of the
soft chimes of
the laughter that is exclusively yours, and
the muted hand-waved-away exclamations
that so effectively consign
ghoulish problems to
oblivion and nothingness.

Yet
that was no laughing matter,
my dear,
it was not at all funny:

The Hospital was sinking,
has since been abandoned,
and not replaced.

Don't ask me where the patients
    are who should have been there.

    But
    the poem
    refused to work –

    That poem had refused to pull
                    itself together
    then

    and in time,
    its many loose parts crumbled.

    Like the revolution that refused to take off!

'No wonder,'
I say to myself now
at a time and from a place
quite far away and strangely near.

High
on this mountain
where the air
is dry, and
the sound of the sea
is heard only rarely in
travellers tales and
the lore of returning warriors,

I think of you.

I see you and
call back into being
the poem that would not work.

It comes:

gathers itself up
pieces cranking themselves into place,
slowly at first, like
my phoenix rising.
Then a roar like jet.

It comes:

flapping its fish-eagle wings
'No problem now,' it says.

'The subject, is
here,
and now.'

A Path in the Sky

I swear
I saw this morning
a path in the sky
where
Clouds had parted for an
aeroplane
to pass.

They looked like
they had done the best they could:

arranged themselves
in orderly ridges,
like those Amadu used to make for his yams.

No Cloud
could really believe it
the first time it occurred.

They too
had thought
they were in
a nicely noisy smoky hot
nightmare...

O, those metal monsters
kept coming and going.
Their numbers and frequency
grew rapidly with time.

Until the Clouds
too
came to accept that
the world they knew was gone.

So,
now that
such enforced paths are
a permanent feature of the sky

they wonder
how humans who made the
morning fires
        rising
        falling
        retreating,
        advancing
        gliding
        diving
can find it quite possible to

complain
without end about
droughts
        and floods
                and what-else
without end.

The Clouds could say it is:

double-think
double-talk
double-everything.

But that too is a human invention!

3 a.m. and Airborne
– *for Kinna V*

WHO SAID...

...that
the world has
changed?

Time has not, nor
distances. And
certainly not our
desires.

We came with
old curiosities;
a slightly updated greed,
searching for gold, or
more contemporary metals

– and useful minds to use.

Then there is
Knowledge.
Knowledge healthy
knowledge dangerous
but
knowledge
knowledge
knowledge.

Yet
some wanderers
look for no more than
their own souls and other
                    kindred hearts.

And if
we traversed
7000 miles in 7 hours,
– or some such computation –
we did nothing
grandmother and grandfather
did not do much better...

Me Ba
we know so little of
how air travel
really affects us.

Except that such
concentrated fear and nervousness
must
permanently

our bodies batter
our cells reduce
our minds ruin.

We know only that
we take the same time to recover
if ever...

as they did,
when they
trudged forestways
waded through dangerous streams
swam hostile rivers
used up desert days
and
sweated through swampy nights.

On feet
wore out precious bottoms
and even more precious
camel's back.

Even Beans Have Skins!

... They'd been
rid of last minute jetsam
washed – three times at least – mind you,

soaked
boiled
– absolutely soft –

cooled and drained
or drained and cooled,
portioned.

So these were really
the frozen leftovers.

And we daren't consider the many other processes
they'd been through
since the morning
each bean sprouted
the green delicate leaves

its job done and fruit shrivelled to look like

Little Fatumata's dainty purple womanhood
the morning before
M'ma Kasuwa came to
infibulate.

And now
defrosted
heated
skins in shreds and ready for the table,

I can see
the separate pieces of each

shredded silken skin
soft as mimosas
alive, in the rain.

And I think
they are saying goodbye...

A Birthday Gift
– *for Mumbi (Mugo)*

Take this gift, My Child,
it is not much.
Just a bowl of petals:

possibly coloured,
dried and scented
artificially.

It serves no purpose.

Except to bring
– when the breezes blow where they should,
which is rare these days –

a whiff of
old forest goodness and
modern garden freshness...so called.

But enjoy it if you can.

In full knowledge   that
it is just the kind of
not-so-useful gift

I would have loved
when I was then as
you are now.

Take this gift,
My Child,
it is for you.

A Postcard From My Vacation
– *for Micere Mugo (II)*

My Sister,

you and I have agreed that
if I had had the money,
I should now be
in the Azores.

Or at least, Mauritius.

Soaking in the sun,   and
covering up my arse
with extra melanin, which, thank God,
yours truly does not need.

So I lie here in Njeri's room,

sleeping the fatigue of
years of questionable
upping and downing,
to-ing and fro-ing.

When I wake up, it is
to read what I wish,
not what I must.
Which makes the difference,

and to crunch up
extra calories, which,
more gratitude to God,
yours truly truly does not need.

I suspect that
from the richer and more precise

world of those who know how
to describe us better than we do ourselves,

this is an excellent
Poor African Woman's Holiday.

Thank you for the space,
and so much else.

Back to Square Zero Plus

Burgled out of half my recent life's work
which no thief,
however ingenious can make a cent out of,
being bits of paper really,

thrown out of
the mean ole hole
I did not own but was clearly
the only home I had,

I yell out like
I must have yelled
the day I was born, from horror of
total nakedness and utter exposure.

But my mama was then
somewhere in the neighbourhood.
Today she is
a few thousand miles away.

Plus,
who wants to listen to
anyone's almost- 50-year-old baby
crying?!

June 7, 1989

– *for Baby Ekua Marguerite Prah (II)*

'Nsu kyer ahina m'aa, obon!'

This
is what the ancients said:

that
the purest water
turns stale,
for standing too long in
a bottle
a gourd.

They spoke out then.

And truly thanks to you,

I sit here
perched over
Boston,
in this
plush post-modernist penthouse,

watching a
120-channel TV set, and
looking for a small
soothsayer's stone
to hand to them
today.

So how did I come to
ever
think of this
bunch of doddering
old strangers as my allies?

And my ancestors replied:
Hen Nana listen:

Their wisdom has atrophied through
too much
power handled
too long with
too much certainty.

A Revelation

'Ask whatsoever in my name, and I shall do it.'

I saw these words or those amounting to same
in a shop window that promised solace to a
bewildered me and my world.

'What a fantastical promise!' I thought.

So here is to a humbler me who sees:

the point in being God must be the power to
   say this, and more, and do.

Woman

– for Kinna (X): on her 21st birthday
(– originally meant to be a very private poem not quite finished)

That's what the West say
You become today.

What a laugh.

Starting from some
African definitions of
Womanhood,
Your journey here has been
decade-long at least:

Marked by
pebbles;
stones;   and a
boulder, or two, that
you hit or which nearly hit you
along the way.

There were plenty of good things
                and glorious too
– also along the way.

May you be blessed manifold
or better still, woman (i) fold.

Adjoa,
You are your father's and
your mother's daugther.

But if you ever doubted it
– and I don't see why
                you ever should–!

feel the heat of
your inquiring chemist's mind
that glows, so far, like a
miniature crystalline volcano;
your restlessly sorrowing heart
                              that
would, if it could,
heal all of the world's wounds
in a day

and your sweet stubborn imagination
that bobs up here and there
                        every now and then:
a jaunty cork on life's waters
refusing to be drowned
against your trying.

Relax, my love and enjoy
your double helix.

Your roots
literally
tap through
the depth and the width of
an entire continent.

Me Ba,
na wommpe wei,
na wope dien?

I confess
You need no prodding to
accept
enjoy and
fight
for your inheritance.

For the rest
My dear Young Woman,

Me sre,
Nana Twerampon na
Asaase Efua

(and not forgetting the best of your Ancestors
of East and West Africa)

de :
Wo mboa w',
Wo nhyira w',

May They help you
be, and stay
Wise;
Vision clear
at all times
in all places

intelligent and
courageous.

May you always be
healthy too: in
body
mind   and
spirit.

Me Ba,
wo tsir nkwa.

Afenhyiapa o!

Notes

including an attempt to place and date each poem

I have recently had to admit that nearly all the poems I write are statements I would like to make, or wish I had made, to friends and relatives: either as a contribution to a discussion, a reply to some query, a complaint, an appreciation, etc. etc. This is really because, I suspect, I am one of those people who go away from encounters only to remember later (much much later!) all the brilliant remarks they should have made to the other party. That should also probably explain why Kinna, who is my daughter and the person closest to me, has had more than a lion's share of poems dedicated to her...

In any case, it has occurred to me that the honest thing to do would be to acknowledge publicly the identity of the individuals or groups who had 'inspired' each poem, wherever applicable. This had not been too clear to me when my first collection of poems was being published (*Someone Talking to Sometime*. Harare: College Press, 1985). So the attempt to identify the dedicatees at that time had been somewhat half-hearted, with people often referred to by their first names only. I have decided to be more open in *Angry Letter*... Therefore, in nearly all cases, names are given in full, or at least people's last names are put in brackets.

As Always, a Painful Declaration of Independence. Glasgow (Scotland) September 21, 1991.

Images of Africa at Century's End. Harare (Zimbabwe) July 1, 1991.
Whopei! Abae-o-o-o! – Akan (Ghana), exclamations expressing dismay, shock, wonderment and sometimes, warning. Compare with later on in the same poem, the exclamations below.
Enfin! Hélas!! Mon Dieux!!! – French, translating roughly as 'Finally! Alas!! My God!!!
Ebusuafo – Akan clan hailing normally used during critical times and at other gatherings.
Wekumei – This (Ga, Ghana) and *Ebusuafo* translate directly into one another and are used in more or less the same situations.

In Memoriam: The Ghana Drama Studio. Harare, July 1, 1990.

A Question From the Expatriate Community. Harare, July 4, 1990.

An Angry Letter in January. Harare, March 14, 1990.

Speaking of Hurricanes. Harare, October 15, 1989.
June 7, 1989, on Tiananmen Square. Brookline Village (Massachusetts, USA) June 10, 1989.

Mo Nua – Akan for 'My Sister' in this context, or in others, 'My Brother'.
Gotta-gotta – Ghanaian pidgin for a form of urban youngster's soccer. It acquired its name from the fact that normally, the teams played in an open space between two huge open drains or gutters. (Gifts from insensitive colonial and neo-colonial civil planners and engineers.) Goal posts were not necessary, since it was considered that a goal had been scored if the ball fell into either of the gutters. As long as the figures were equal, the opposing teams could be made up of any numbers between one and eleven. No doubt, part of the thrill was that the children always knew the game was dangerous, since the chances of not only the ball but of they themselves falling into the gutters were always great.
Ampe – A girls' jump-and-clap game (Ghana). There are different forms of it. But the central rule was always the same. You had to co-ordinate clapping hands with agreed leg-work. If a player missed, it went against her and her team, when there were more than one player on each side.

These Days. Harare, March 10, 1990.
Moboso gya. Mammbohwe wo nkwan m'. Literally, 'I only came to borrow a few live coals from your fire. I never meant to stare into your soup.' In this context the speaking voice is asking to be excused. She'd meant a question literally, and not as a pretext to get to know other folks' family business.

A Modern African Story. Harare, March 10, 1990.

Questions. Harare (Zimbabwe)/Richmond, Virginia (USA), August 1986/January 1989.

New in Africa: I. Harare, October 14, 1989.
Shamwari – Chi-Shona (Zimbabwe) expression, meaning 'friend'.

New in Africa: II. Harare, October 31, 1989.

New in Africa: III. Harare, July 5, 1989.

Not So New in Africa. Harare, October 14, 1989.

Loving the Black Angel. Harare, October 28, 1985.
The Genesis of 'Loving the Black Angel'

Although I had known that I might read at an evening of readings organized in memory of Alex La Guma and Ben Moloise by the Zimbabwe Writers' Union, I was not going to try and write a brand new poem for the occasion. How could I? It was only a week after the hanging of Moloise, and one had been trained on the idea that poetry can only issue from **'emotions recollected in tranquillity'**. Besides, I knew quite well that all we felt at this murder was **RAGE**, and there was no way I, or anyone else on our side of the battle lines, could claim then, or ever, that we had become tranquil enough about it to **'recollect'** our emotions and write a poem. However, that was to change at dawn on 25th October, the day of the readings. It occurred to me that if that notion of the genesis of poetry had never really sounded right to me before, it definitely sounded all wrong then. For instance, if we had organized a wake for our fallen heroes according to our own customs and traditions, then those of us who were recognized by the community as being poets would definitely be expected to produce poetry for the occasion, and our best at that. So in the morning, I very humbly took my pen, and the following is what I was able to do.

It should be rough, this poem, for after all, it did not emanate from emotions recollected anywhere near 'tranquillity'.
Harare: 28 October, 1985.

On Seeing a Small U.S. Airforce Plane at Luanda Airport, June 1987. Harare, June 29, 1987.

After a Commonwealth Conference. Harare, June 19, 1986. (Needless to say, this was written after the Vancouver CHOGM, not Harare's, which came later in 1991.)

No Grief No Joy. Harare, June 19, 1986.

Compromise. Harare, July 19, 1986.

An Insider's View. Harare, November 8, 1989.
Suminado – (Akan) 'rubbish dump' normally at the outskirts of the village.

Homesickness. Sydney (Australia), November 1989.
Fantse – A central coastal dialect of Akan as identified by the people who speak it. Non-speakers call it 'Fanti'. Also compare *Asante* and 'Ashanti'.

At Mokador: I. Harare, October 23, 1989.

At Mokador: II. Harare, October 27, 1989.

Family. Kalamazoo, Michigan, USA, August 11, 1988.

After an Argument. Harare, January 30, 1990.
Ndugu – Ki-Swahili (Kenya/Tanzania/Uganda, etc.) meaning: 'Big' or 'Respected' Brother.

In Salute to an Enemy of Sorts. Harare, June 30, 1990.
Apa – Akan. Specially constructed, often bamboo, large shelf for holding farm produce. Strictly rural.

Just One More Job for Mama. Brookline Village, January 2, 1989.
Ajumako ampesi wobo kaw dzi – Literally, 'You have to spend money to eat at Ajumako'. Ajumako is a small rural town in south-central Ghana and one of the strategic stops on the 'old Accra road' or the old main east-

west artery of coastal Ghana. It was also one of the points where the people of that particular region experienced the trauma of colonial urbanization with its endemic meannesses, 'cash-for-everything', including meals, whereas in the old old days in the villages, a meal was considered 'free' because it was prepared from produce that people grew on their farms, or from easy gifts from relatives, friends, and neighbours.

Mara mo ndue – Akan. Swearing an oath derived from a personal or collective calamity (as in 'my wounded knee') is a way of publicly proclaiming oneself to be speaking an indisputable truth. The accepted convention was that on hearing such an oath spoken, someone present should cry out 'due!' as an expression of sympathy and understanding. In this poem I am swearing my personal oath and crying out for myself at the same time!

Motherhood and the Numbers Game. Harare, July 1989.
The first three lines of the poem is only a rephrasing of the lines in Fantse, which literally mean 'thank you, thank you, thank you. Thank you for letting me know (by harrassing me on account of my daughter) that I too am a mother.'

Whom Do We Thank for Women's Conferences? Moscow (USSR), June 27, 1987.

A Young Woman's Voice Doesn't Break. It Gets Firmer. Moscow, June 26/27, 1987.

Comparisons II: We Women, Still! The Pier, University of Richmond, Richmond (Virginia, USA), May 16/17, 1989.

These Days: II. Harare, February 8, 1991.

Guest Accommodation. Stony Brook (New York, USA), October 30, 1989.

Funny Standards. Brookline Village, June 11, 1989.

July 19, 1989. Harare, July 21, 1989.

Path in the Sky. Between Moscow and Harare, June 29, 1987.

3 a.m. and Airborne. Between Moscow and Harare, June 29, 1987.
Me Ba – Akan for 'My Child'.

Even Beans Have Skins! Harare, January 1990.

A Birthday Gift. Harare, October 13-14, 1989.

A Postcard From My Vacation. Harare, November 10, 1989.

Back to Square Zero Plus. Harare, November 14, 1989.

June 7, 1989. Brookline Village, June 10, 1989.

A Revelation. Harare, December 3, 1989.

Woman. London (England), December 9, 1990.